Fast & Festive
50 CHRISTMAS DESIGNS
From The Design Works Crafts, Inc. Collection

Table of Contents

Angel • Candles 3
Cat and Stocking • Cat in Hat 4
Christmas Blessings • Flying Angel 5
Joy • Juggling Penguin 6
Sampler • Santa and Snowman 7
Santa Cheers • Santa in Sled 8
Santa on Roof • Santa with Candle 9
Santa with List • Santa with Wreath 10
Santa on Sled • Sitting Teddy 11
Sledding Teddy • Snowlady 12
Snowman and Bunny • Snowman and Deer 13
Cat and Mouse • Tree 14
Cat in Present • Cat in Wreath 15
Cat with Tree • Dreaming Mouse 18
Doorway Wreath • Ho Ho Ho Santa 19
Joy Cat • Kitty 20
Laughing Teddy • Merry Christmas 21
Mouse with Toys • Noel 22
Noel Teddy • Peace Angel 23
Penguin and Snowman • Poinsettia 24
Puppy • Santa 25
Santa's Book • Santa and Puppy 26
Santa and Teddy • Santa and Toy Bag 27
Skating Teddy • Teddy and Soldier 28
Teddy and Reindeer • Teddy Tree 29
General Instructions 30

Leisure Arts Inc. • Maumelle Arkansas

SEASON'S
GREETINGS
CHEER

Jolly
Holidays

ANGEL (43w x 58h)

X	DMC	1/4X	B'ST	ANC.	COLOR
	blanc			2	white
	350			11	coral
	434			310	dk tan
	436			1045	lt tan
	676			891	lt gold
	677			886	vy lt gold
	702			226	green
	704			256	lt green
	817			13	dk coral
	928			274	lt blue grey
	951			1010	lt flesh
	3326			36	pink
	3371			382	brown black
	350			11	coral Fr. Knot
	3371			382	brown black Fr. Knot
					Kreinik Very Fine (#4) Braid #002 gold

Kreinik Very Fine (#4) Braid #002 gold Fr. Knot

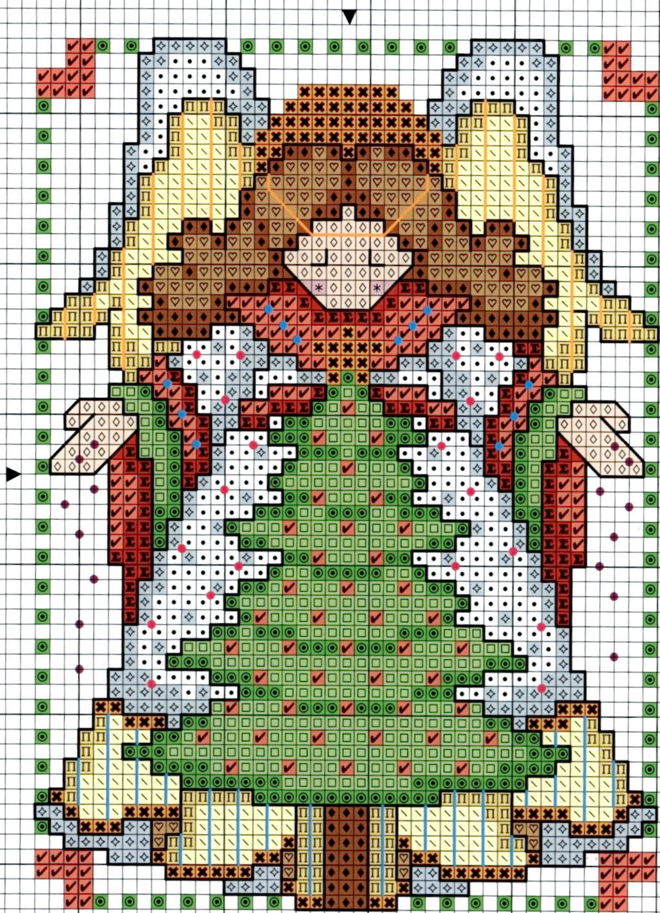

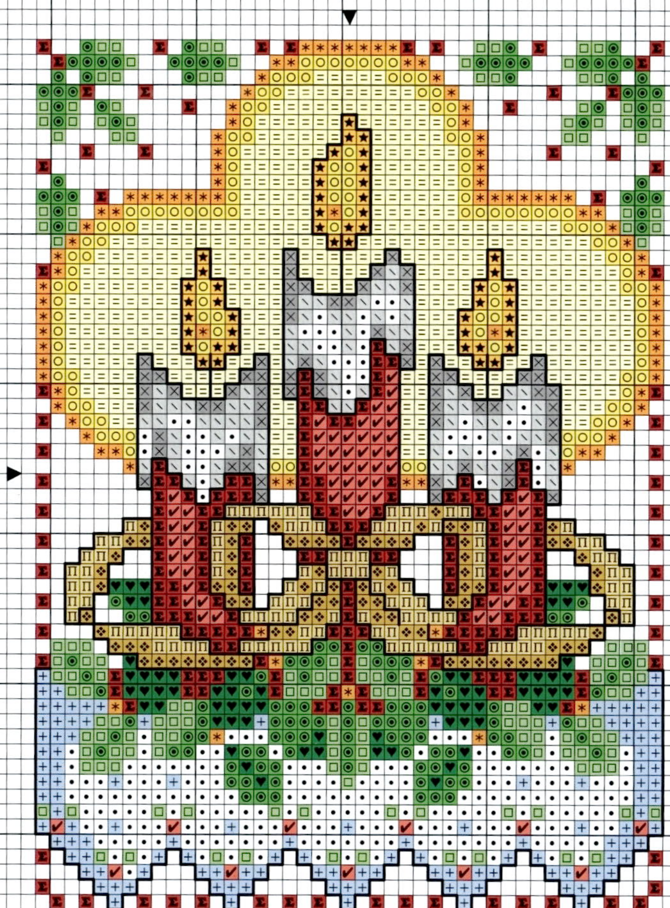

CANDLES (43w x 58h)

X	DMC	B'ST	ANC.	COLOR
	blanc		2	white
	350		11	coral
	415		398	lt grey
	676		891	lt gold
	699		923	dk green
	702		226	green
	704		256	lt green
	729		890	gold
	742		303	dk gold
	743		302	yellow
	745		300	lt yellow
	762		234	vy lt grey
	817		13	dk coral
	828		9159	vy lt blue
	3371		382	brown black

Kreinik Very Fine (#4) Braid #002 gold

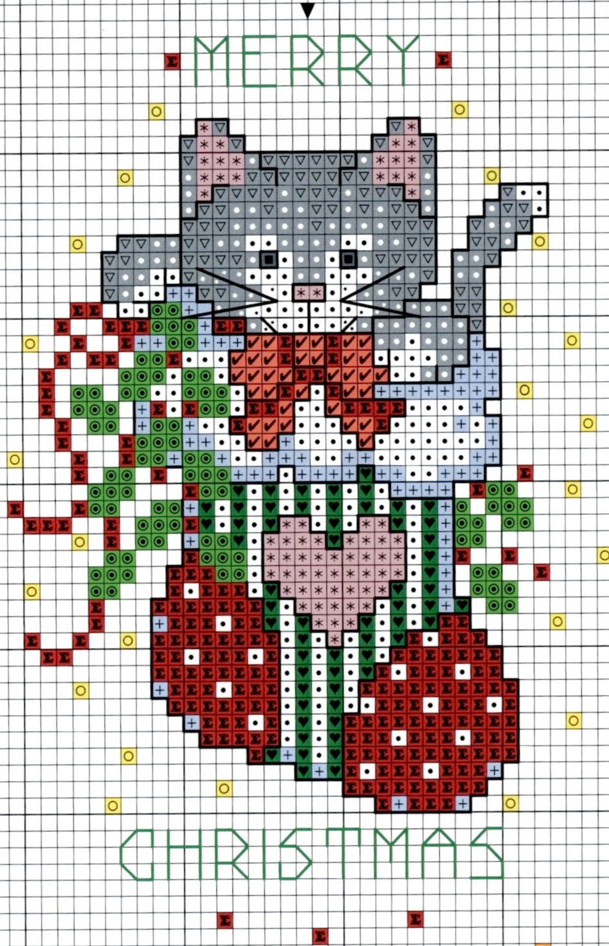

CAT AND STOCKING (38w x 55h)

X	DMC	B'ST	ANC.	COLOR
	blanc		2	white
	310	/ *	403	black
	317		400	dk grey
	318		399	grey
	350		11	coral
	699	/	923	dk green
	702		226	green
	726		295	lt topaz
	813		161	lt blue
	817		13	dk coral
	3326		36	pink

* Use long stitches for whiskers.

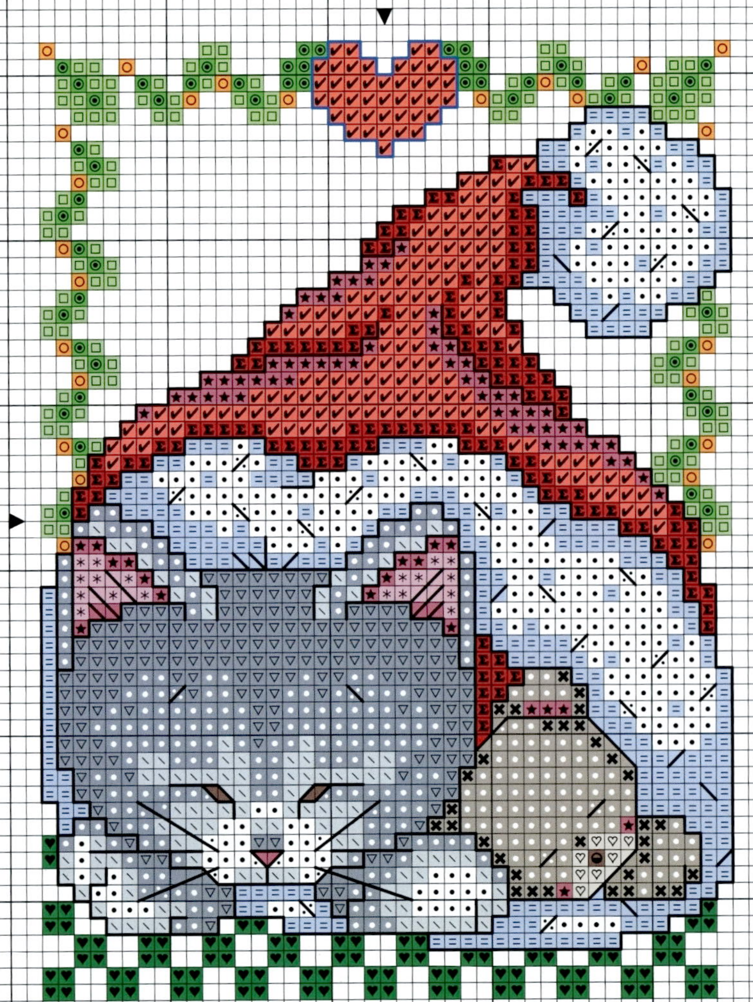

CAT IN HAT (43w x 58h)

X	DMC	1/4X	B'ST	ANC.	COLOR
	blanc			2	white
	317			400	dk grey
	318			399	grey
	350			11	coral
	415			398	lt grey
	699			923	dk green
	702			226	green
	704			256	lt green
	817			13	dk coral
	828			9159	vy lt blue
	899			52	dk pink
	3045			888	dk yellow beige
	3046			887	yellow beige
	3047			852	lt yellow beige
	3326			36	pink
	3371		/ *	382	brown black
			/		Kreinik Very Fine (#4) Braid #002 gold

* Use long stitches for whiskers.

CHRISTMAS BLESSINGS (43w x 58h)

X	DMC	B'ST	ANC.	COLOR
•	blanc		2	white
■	310	/	403	black
✔	350		11	coral
▽	436		1045	lt tan
♥	699	/	923	dk green
◉	702		226	green
◇	726		295	lt topaz
Σ	817		13	dk coral
*	3326		36	pink
•	699		923	dk green Fr. Knot

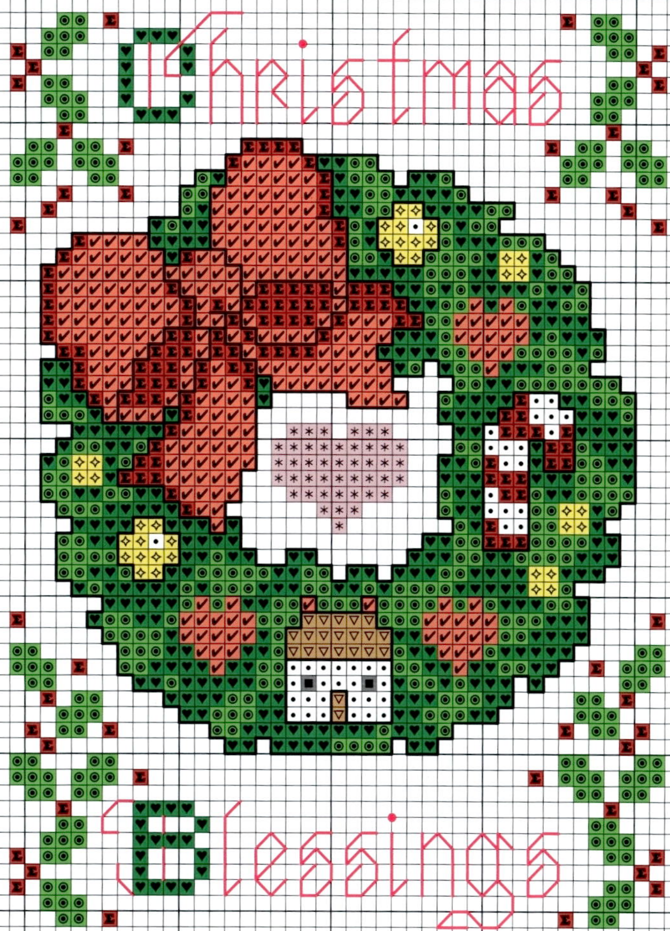

FLYING ANGEL (43w x 58h)

X	DMC	1/4X	B'ST	ANC.	COLOR
•	blanc			2	white
✔	350	◢		11	coral
◆	434	◢		310	dk tan
▽	436	◢		1045	lt tan
Π	676			891	lt gold
O	677			886	vy lt gold
♥	699	◢	/	923	dk green
◉	702	◢		226	green
⬠	813	◢		161	lt blue
Σ	817			13	dk coral
+	828			9159	vy lt blue
✕	928			274	lt blue grey
\	951	◢		1010	lt flesh
*	3326			36	pink
⊠	3371	◢	/	382	brown black
☆			/		Kreinik Very Fine (#4) Braid #002 gold

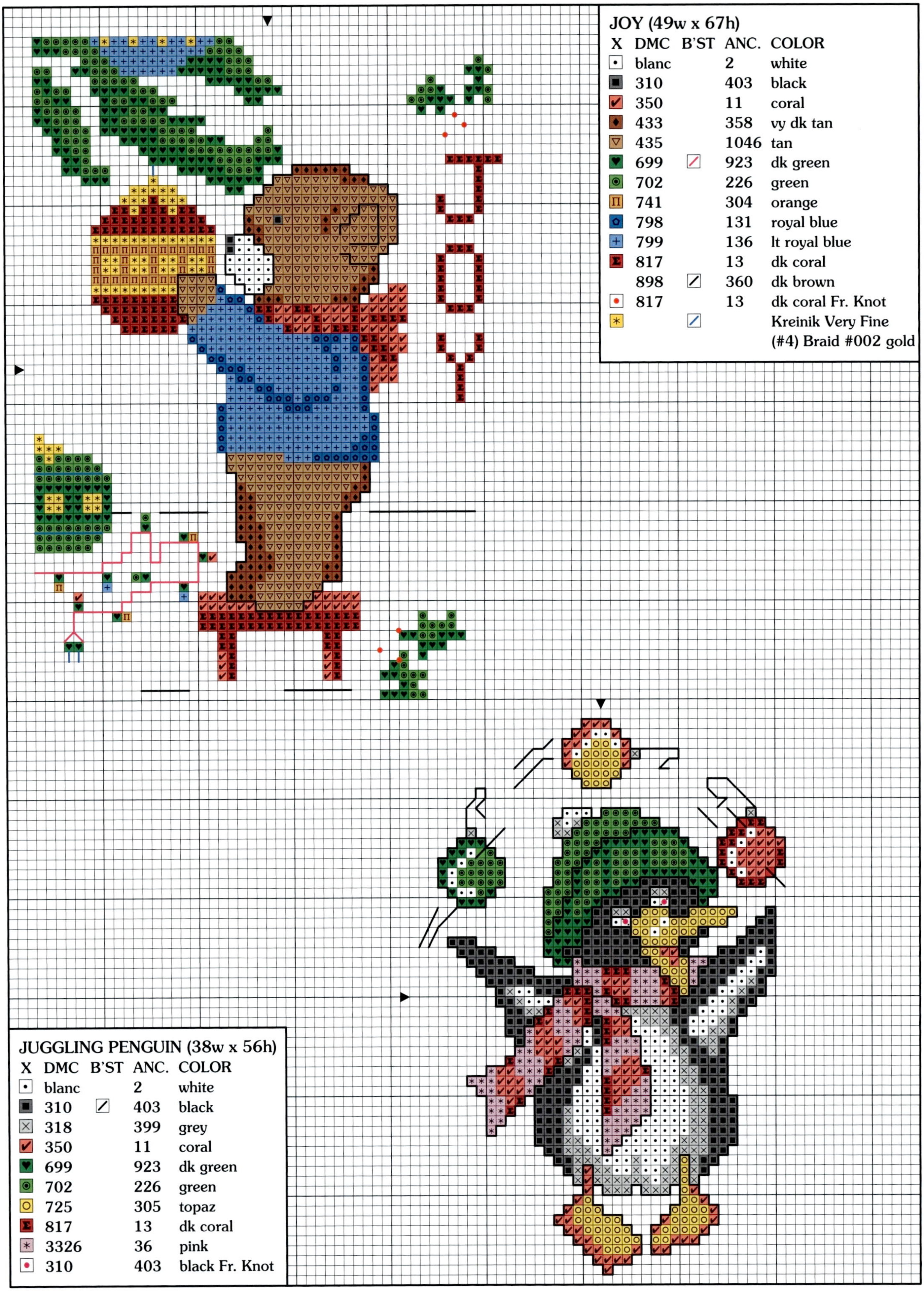

JOY (49w x 67h)

X	DMC	B'ST	ANC.	COLOR
•	blanc		2	white
■	310		403	black
✔	350		11	coral
♦	433		358	vy dk tan
▽	435		1046	tan
♥	699	/	923	dk green
◎	702		226	green
Π	741		304	orange
⬠	798		131	royal blue
+	799		136	lt royal blue
Σ	817		13	dk coral
	898	/	360	dk brown
•	817		13	dk coral Fr. Knot
*		/		Kreinik Very Fine (#4) Braid #002 gold

JUGGLING PENGUIN (38w x 56h)

X	DMC	B'ST	ANC.	COLOR
•	blanc		2	white
■	310	/	403	black
✕	318		399	grey
✔	350		11	coral
♥	699		923	dk green
◎	702		226	green
○	725		305	topaz
Σ	817		13	dk coral
*	3326		36	pink
•	310		403	black Fr. Knot

SAMPLER (43w x 58h)

X	DMC	B'ST	ANC.	COLOR
•	blanc		2	white
▼	311		148	dk blue
Π	334		977	blue
✔	350		11	coral
♥	699		923	dk green
◉	702		226	green
★	742		303	dk yellow
○	743		302	yellow
=	745		300	lt yellow
Σ	817		13	dk coral
+	828		9159	vy lt blue
♡	3023			brown grey
✖	3045		888	dk yellow beige
▫	3046		887	yellow beige
●	3371	⁄	382	brown black
*	Kreinik Very Fine (#4) Braid #002 gold			

SANTA AND SNOWMAN (51w x 58h)

X	DMC	B'ST	ANC.	COLOR
•	blanc		2	white
■	310	⁄*	403	black
✔	350		11	coral
✕	415		398	lt grey
▽	420		374	hazel brown
✧	676		891	lt gold
♥	699		923	dk green
◉	702		226	green
□	704		256	lt green
○	725		305	topaz
Π	729		890	gold
⬠	741		304	orange
ǁ	813		161	lt blue
Σ	817		13	dk coral
⟍	945		881	flesh
✳	3326		36	pink
•	310		403	black Fr. Knot

* Use long stitches for broom straws.

SANTA CHEERS (34w x 47h)

X	DMC	B'ST	ANC.	COLOR
	blanc		2	white
	310	/	403	black
	317	/	400	dk grey
	350		11	coral
	699		923	dk green
	702		226	green
	813		161	lt blue
	817		13	dk coral
	945		881	flesh
	951		1010	lt flesh
	976		1001	copper
	310		403	black Fr. Knot
	Kreinik Very Fine (#4) Braid #002 gold			

SANTA IN SLED (45w x 57h)

X	DMC	B'ST	ANC.	COLOR
	blanc		2	white
	310	/	403	black
	350		11	coral
	415		398	lt grey
	435		1046	tan
	436		1045	lt tan
	676		891	lt gold
	699		923	dk green
	702		226	green
	704		256	lt green
	725		305	topaz
	813		161	lt blue
	817	/	13	dk coral
	945		881	flesh
	3326		36	pink
	310		403	black Fr. Knot

SANTA ON ROOF (43w x 58h)

X	DMC	1/4X	B'ST	ANC.	COLOR
	blanc			2	white
	310			403	black
	350			11	coral
	415			398	lt grey
	699			923	dk green
	702			226	green
	704			256	lt green
	726			295	lt topaz
	762			234	vy lt grey
	817			13	dk coral
	828			9159	vy lt blue
	945			881	flesh
	951			1010	lt flesh
	3045			888	dk yellow beige
	3046			887	yellow beige
	3326			36	pink
	310			403	black Fr. Knot
	Kreinik Very Fine (#4) Braid #002 gold				

SANTA WITH CANDLE (43w x 58h)

X	DMC	1/4X	B'ST	ANC.	COLOR
	blanc			2	white
	350			11	coral
	415			398	lt grey
	420			374	hazel brown
	702			226	green
	704			256	lt green
	725			305	topaz
	726			295	lt topaz
	817			13	dk coral
	828			9159	vy lt blue
	945			881	flesh
	951			1010	lt flesh
	3045			888	dk yellow beige
	3371			382	brown black
	3371			382	brown black Fr. Knot
	Kreinik Very Fine (#4) Braid #002 gold				

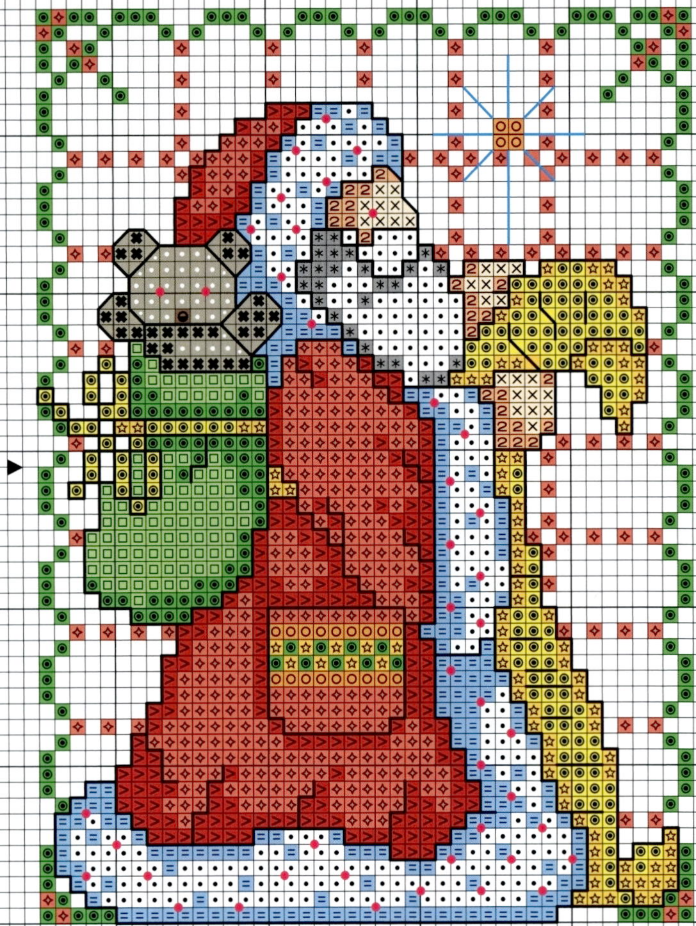

SANTA WITH LIST (43w x 58h)

X	DMC	¼X	B'ST	ANC.	COLOR
	blanc			2	white
	350			11	coral
	415			398	lt grey
	702			226	green
	704			256	lt green
	725			305	topaz
	726			295	lt topaz
	817			13	dk coral
	828			9159	vy lt blue
	945			881	flesh
	951			1010	lt flesh
	3045			888	dk yellow beige
	3046			887	yellow beige
	3371			382	brown black
	3371			382	brown black Fr. Knot
			*		Kreinik Very Fine (#4) Braid #002 gold

*Use long stitches.

SANTA WITH WREATH (43w x 58h)

X	DMC	B'ST	ANC.	COLOR
	blanc		2	white
	350		11	coral
	415		398	lt grey
	702		226	green
	704		256	lt green
	725		305	topaz
	726		295	lt topaz
	817		13	dk coral
	828		9159	vy lt blue
	945		881	flesh
	951		1010	lt flesh
	3371		382	brown black
	3371		382	brown black Fr. Knot
	Kreinik Very Fine (#4) Braid #002 gold			

SANTA ON SLED (50w x 70h)

X	DMC	B'ST	ANC.	COLOR
	blanc		2	white
	310		403	black
	318		399	grey
	334		977	blue
	350		11	coral
	415		398	lt grey
	433		358	vy dk tan
	435		1046	tan
	436		1045	lt tan
	699	*	923	dk green
	702		226	green
	726		295	lt topaz
	813		161	lt blue
	815		43	dk coral
	817		13	red
	945		881	flesh
	3326		36	pink
	*699		923	dk green Fr. Knot
				Kreinik Very Fine (#4) Braid #001 silver
				Kreinik Very Fine (#4) Braid #002 gold

*Use an additional strand of floss for wording

SITTING TEDDY (43w x 58h)

X	DMC	1/4X	3/4X	B'ST	ANC.	COLOR
	blanc				2	white
	350				11	coral
	699				923	dk green
	702				226	green
	704				256	lt green
	742				303	dk yellow
	743				302	yellow
	817				13	dk coral
	828				9159	vy lt blue
	3045				888	dk yellow beige
	3046				887	yellow beige
	3047				852	lt yellow beige
	3326				36	pink
	3371				382	brown black
	3371				382	brown black Fr. Knot
	Kreinik Very Fine (#4) Braid #002 gold					

SLEDDING TEDDY (42w x 57h)

X	DMC	B'ST	ANC.	COLOR
■	310	/	403	black
✔	350		11	coral
Π	676		891	lt gold
✖	680		901	dk gold
♥	699		923	dk green
◎	702		226	green
□	704		256	lt green
✦	729		890	gold
+	813		161	lt blue
●	817	/*	13	dk coral
*	3326		36	pink
•	817		13	dk coral Fr. Knot

* Use an additional strand of floss.

SNOWLADY (41w x 53h)

X	DMC	1/4X	B'ST	ANC.	COLOR
•	blanc	◺		2	white
	310		/	403	black
✕	415		/	398	lt grey
◆	436			1045	lt tan
Σ	498			1005	red
♥	699		/	923	dk green
◎	702			226	green
⊖	741	◢		304	orange
+	813			161	lt blue
●	817			13	dk coral
*	3326			36	pink
•	blanc			2	white Fr. Knot
•	310			403	black Fr. Knot
•	817			13	dk coral Fr. Knot
			/		Kreinik Very Fine (#4) Braid #001 silver

● Kreinik Very Fine (#4) Braid #001 silver Fr. Knot

SNOWMAN AND BUNNY (43w x 59h)

X	DMC	B'ST	ANC.	COLOR
•	blanc		2	white
■	310	/	403	black
✔	350		11	coral
⊠	415		398	lt grey
▽	676		891	lt gold
♥	699		923	dk green
◎	702		226	green
◆	729		890	gold
Π	741		304	orange
+	813		161	lt blue
▪	817	/	13	dk coral
*	3326		36	pink
•	310		403	black Fr. Knot
•	699		923	dk green Fr. Knot

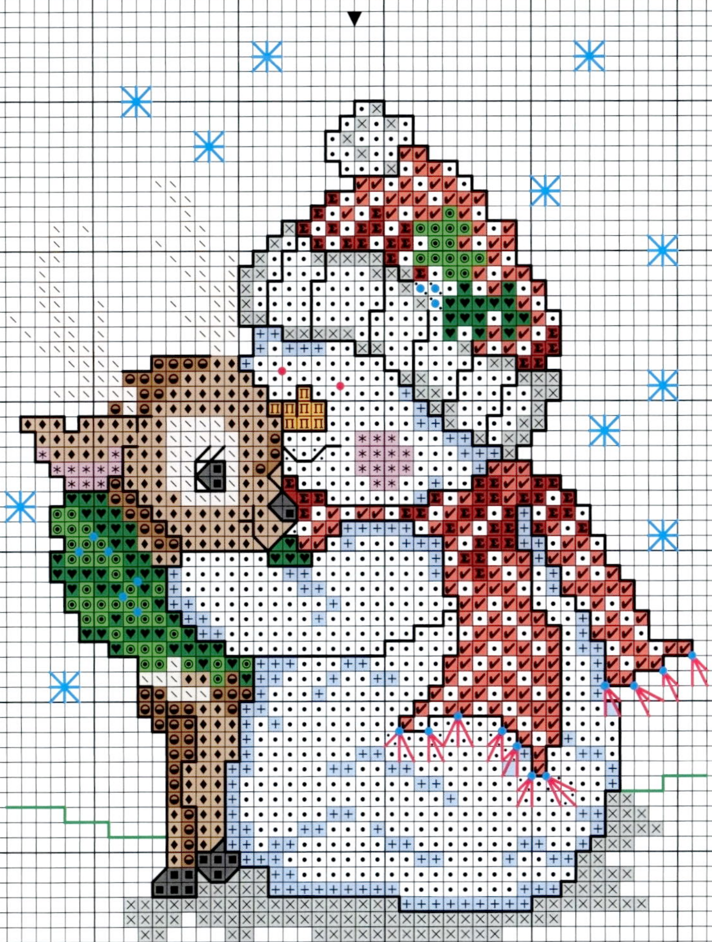

SNOWMAN AND DEER (48w x 60h)

X	DMC	1/4X	B'ST	ANC.	COLOR
•	blanc	◺		2	white
■	310	◢	/	403	black
⊠	415	◢	/	398	lt grey
◒	434	◢		310	dk tan
◆	436	◢		1045	lt tan
Σ	498	◢		1005	red
♥	699	◢		923	dk green
◎	702			226	green
\	739	□		387	vy lt tan
Π	741			304	orange
+	813			161	lt blue
✔	817		/	13	dk coral
*	3326			36	pink
•	310			403	black Fr. Knot
•	817			13	dk coral Fr. Knot
			/		Kreinik Very Fine (#4) Braid #001 silver

CAT AND MOUSE (36w x 57h)

X	DMC	B'ST	ANC.	COLOR
•	blanc		2	white
■	310	⁄*	403	black
4	317		400	dk grey
★	318		399	grey
◇	350		11	coral
♦	676		891	lt gold
✖	699		923	dk green
◎	702		226	green
P	813		161	lt blue
=	817	⁄	13	dk coral
✳	976		1001	copper
2	3326		36	pink

*Use long stitches for whiskers.

TREE (43w x 58h)

X	DMC	B'ST	ANC.	COLOR
d	350		11	coral
●	699	⁄	923	dk green
▽	702		226	green
⟍	704		256	lt green
✦	742		303	dk yellow
✔	743		302	yellow
✚	817		13	dk coral
▲	3371	⁄	382	brown black
☆	Kreinik Very Fine (#4) Braid #002 gold			

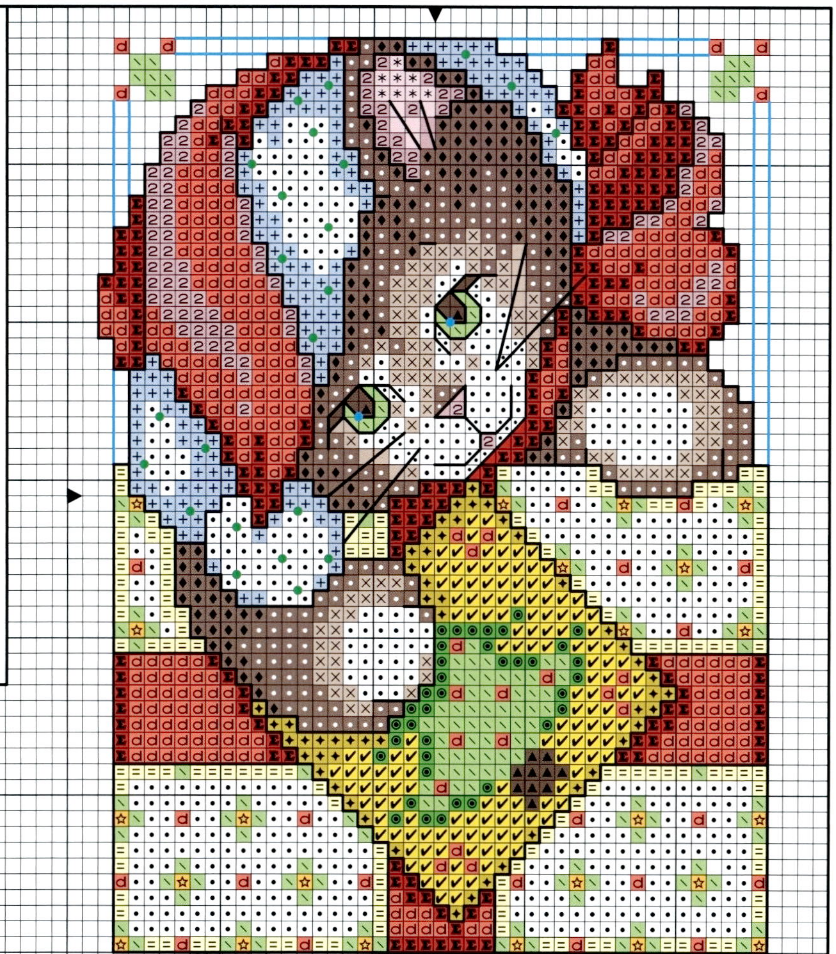

CAT IN PRESENT (44w x 58h)

X	DMC	1/4X	B'ST	ANC.	COLOR
	blanc			2	white
	350			11	coral
	702			226	green
	704			256	lt green
	742			303	dk yellow
	743			302	yellow
	745			300	lt yellow
	817			13	dk coral
	818			23	lt pink
	828			9159	vy lt blue
	3022			393	dk brown grey
	3023				brown grey
	3024			397	lt brown grey
	3326			36	pink
	3371		*	382	brown black
	blanc			2	white Fr. Knot
	3371			382	brown black Fr. Knot
					Kreinik Very Fine (#4) Braid #002 gold

*Use long stitches for whiskers.

CAT IN WREATH (43w x 58h)

X	DMC	1/4X	B'ST	ANC.	COLOR
	blanc			2	white
	350			11	coral
	699			923	dk green
	702			226	green
	704			256	lt green
	725			305	topaz
	783			307	dk topaz
	817			13	dk coral
	899			52	dk pink
	945			881	vy lt copper
	976			1001	copper
	977			1002	lt copper
	3326			36	pink
	3371		*	382	brown black
					Kreinik Very Fine (#4) Braid #002 gold

*Use long stitches for whiskers.

CHEERS
MERRY
CHRISTMAS
CHRISTMAS
IS A SEASON OF
LOVE
GREETINGS
Peace on Earth
NOEL
HO HO HO
JOY

JOY
JOY
GREETINGS
LOVE

CAT WITH TREE (43w x 58h)

X	DMC	1/4X	B'ST	ANC.	COLOR
	blanc			2	white
	350			11	coral
	702			226	green
	704			256	lt green
	817			13	dk coral
	828			9159	vy lt blue
	899			52	dk pink
	945			881	vy lt copper
	976			1001	copper
	977			1002	lt copper
	3326			36	pink
	3371		*	382	brown black
	Kreinik Very Fine (#4) Braid #002 gold				

* Use long stitches for whiskers.

DREAMING MOUSE (43w x 58h)

X	DMC	1/4X	B'ST	ANC.	COLOR
	blanc			2	white
	350			11	coral
	640			903	dk beige grey
	642			392	beige grey
	644			830	lt beige grey
	676			891	lt gold
	680			901	dk gold
	702			226	green
	704			256	lt green
	729			890	gold
	742			303	dk yellow
	743			302	yellow
	817			13	dk coral
	818			23	lt pink
	899			52	dk pink
	927			848	blue grey
	928			274	lt blue grey
	3326			36	pink
	3371			382	brown black
	3371			382	brown black Fr. Knot
	Kreinik Very Fine (#4) Braid #002 gold				

DOORWAY WREATH (43w x 58h)

X	DMC	1/4X	B'ST	ANC.	COLOR
	blanc			2	white
	350			11	coral
	699			923	dk green
	702			226	green
	704			256	lt green
	742			303	dk yellow
	743			302	yellow
	793			176	dk periwinkle
	794			175	periwinkle
	801			359	brown
	817			13	dk coral
	3045			888	dk yellow beige
	3046			887	yellow beige
	3326			36	pink
	3371			382	brown black
	3371			382	brown black Fr. Knot
C	Kreinik Very Fine (#4) Braid #002 gold				

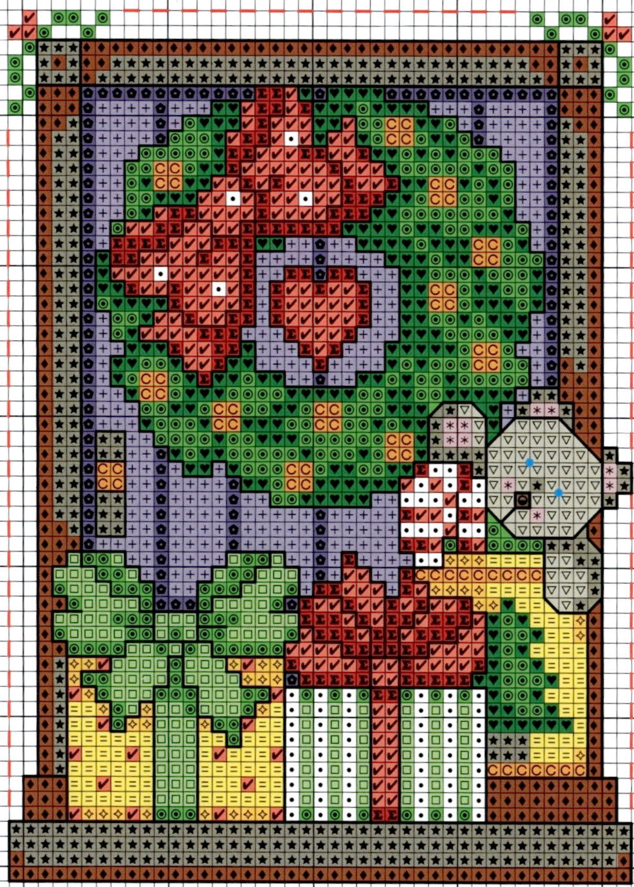

HO HO HO SANTA (49w x 60h)

X	DMC	B'ST	ANC.	COLOR
	blanc		2	white
	310		403	black
	350		11	coral
	415		398	lt grey
	702		226	green
	704		256	lt green
	725		305	topaz
	813		161	lt blue
	817		13	dk coral
	945		881	flesh
	3326		36	pink
	310		403	black Fr. Knot

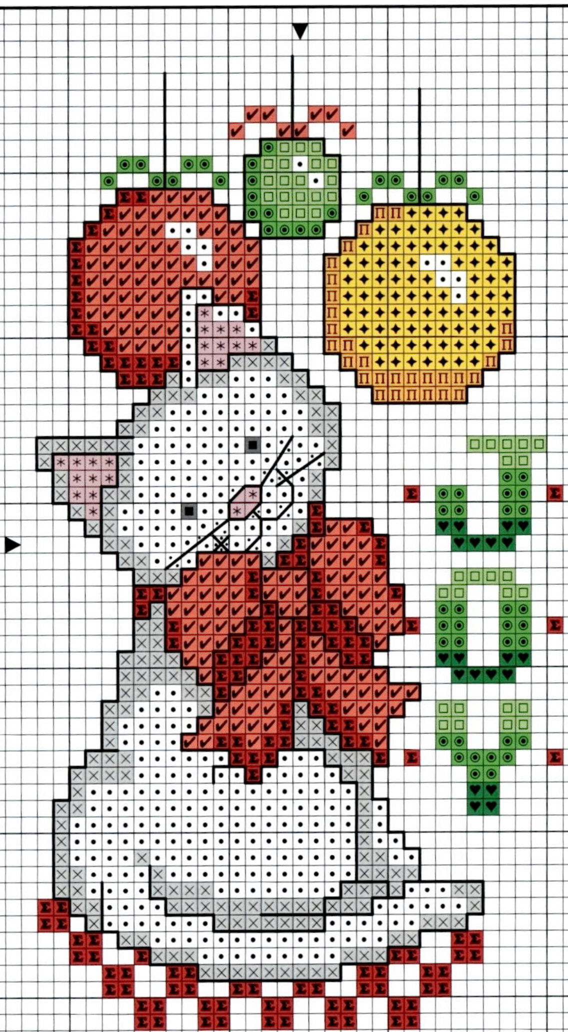

JOY CAT (33w x 59h)

X	DMC	¼X	B'ST	ANC.	COLOR
	blanc	/		2	white
	310		/	403	black
	350			11	coral
	415			398	lt grey
	699			923	dk green
	702			226	green
	704			256	lt green
	741			304	orange
	742			303	dk yellow
	817			13	dk coral
	3326	/		36	pink

KITTY (35w x 55h)

X	DMC	B'ST	ANC.	COLOR
	blanc		2	white
	310	/	403	black
	350		11	coral
	415		398	lt grey
	699	/	923	dk green
	702		226	green
	704		256	lt green
	726		295	lt topaz
	813		161	lt blue
	817		13	dk coral
	3326		36	pink

LAUGHING TEDDY (43w x 58h)

X	DMC	1/4X	B'ST	ANC.	COLOR
	blanc			2	white
	350			11	coral
	702			226	green
	704			256	lt green
	738			361	tan
	742			303	dk yellow
	743			302	yellow
	817			13	dk coral
	828			9159	vy lt blue
	3045			888	dk yellow beige
	3046			887	yellow beige
	3047			852	lt yellow beige
	3326			36	pink
	3371			382	brown black
	3371			382	brown black Fr. Knot
			*		Kreinik Very Fine (#4) Braid #002 gold

* Use long stitches.

MERRY CHRISTMAS (47w x 58h)

X	DMC	B'ST	ANC.	COLOR
	blanc		2	white
	350		11	coral
	699		923	dk green
	702		226	green
	725		305	topaz
	783		307	dk topaz
	817	*	13	dk coral
*	817		13	dk coral Fr. Knot

* Use an additional strand of floss for wording.

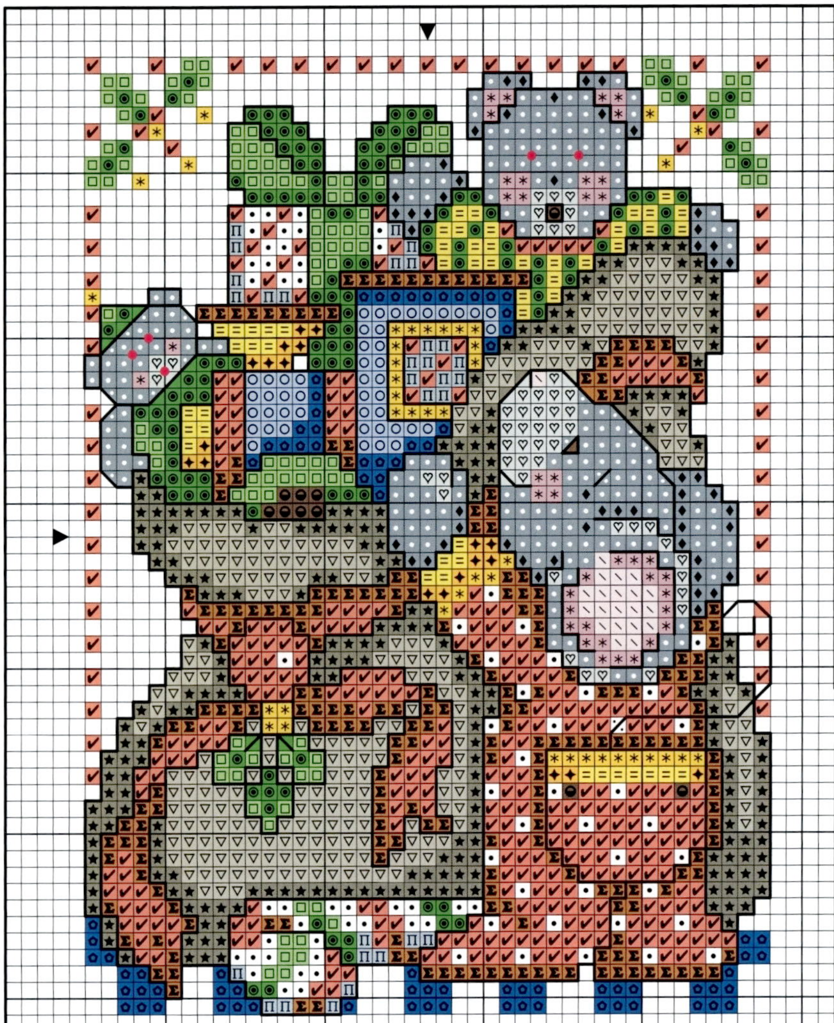

MOUSE WITH TOYS (43w x 58h)

X	DMC	1/4X	B'ST	ANC.	COLOR
	blanc			2	white
	350			11	coral
	640			903	dk beige grey
	642			392	beige grey
	644			830	lt beige grey
	702			226	green
	704			256	lt green
	742			303	dk yellow
	743			302	yellow
	798			131	royal blue
	809			130	lt periwinkle
	817			13	dk coral
	818			23	lt pink
	928			274	lt blue grey
	3045			888	dk yellow beige
	3046			887	yellow beige
	3326			36	pink
	3371			382	brown black
	3371			382	brown black Fr. Knot
	Kreinik Very Fine (#4) Braid #002 gold				

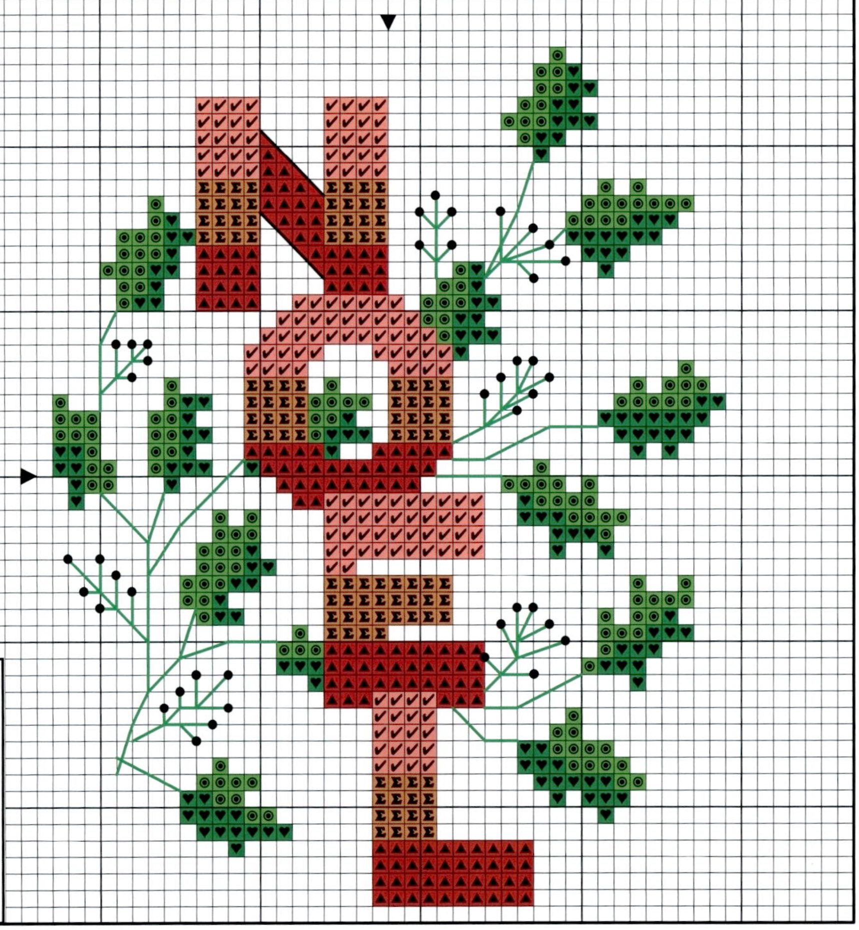

NOEL (42w x 52h)

X	DMC	1/4X	B'ST	ANC.	COLOR
	350			11	coral
	498			1005	red
	699			923	dk green
	702			226	green
	817			13	dk coral
	817			13	dk coral Fr. Knot

NOEL TEDDY (36w x 56h)

X	DMC	1/4X	B'ST	ANC.	COLOR
•	blanc	/		2	white
■	310		/	403	black
⊠	318			399	grey
✓	350			11	coral
◇	676			891	lt gold
✚	680			901	dk gold
♥	699			923	dk green
◉	702			226	green
□	704			256	lt green
•	729			890	gold
Σ	817			13	dk coral
Π	976			1001	copper
*	3326			36	pink
•	310			403	black Fr. Knot
•	817			13	dk coral Fr. Knot

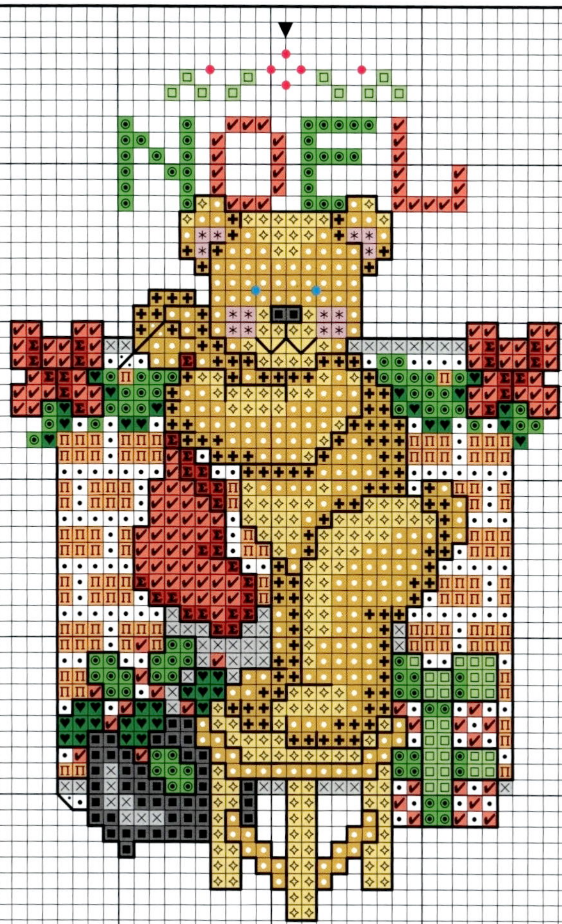

PEACE ANGEL (49w x 58h)

X	DMC	1/4X	B'ST	ANC.	COLOR
•	blanc			2	white
■	310		/	403	black
⊠	318			399	grey
✓	350			11	coral
♥	699			923	dk green
◉	702		/	226	green
□	704	/		256	lt green
○	725			305	topaz
✖	783			307	dk topaz
⁘	813			161	lt blue
Σ	817			13	dk coral
\	945	/		881	flesh
•	310			403	black Fr. Knot
•	702			226	green Fr. Knot
•	817			13	dk coral Fr. Knot

PENGUIN AND SNOWMAN (51w x 67h)

X	DMC	1/4X	B'ST	ANC.	COLOR
	blanc			2	white
	310			403	black
	415			398	lt grey
	676			891	lt gold
	699			923	dk green
	702			226	green
	741			304	orange
	798			131	royal blue
	799			136	lt royal blue
	817			13	dk coral
	976			1001	copper
	3326			36	pink
	blanc			2	white Fr. Knot
	310			403	black Fr. Knot
	699			923	dk green Fr. Knot
	817			13	dk coral Fr. Knot
					Kreinik Very Fine (#4) Braid #001 silver
	Kreinik Very Fine (#4) Braid #001 silver Fr. Knot				

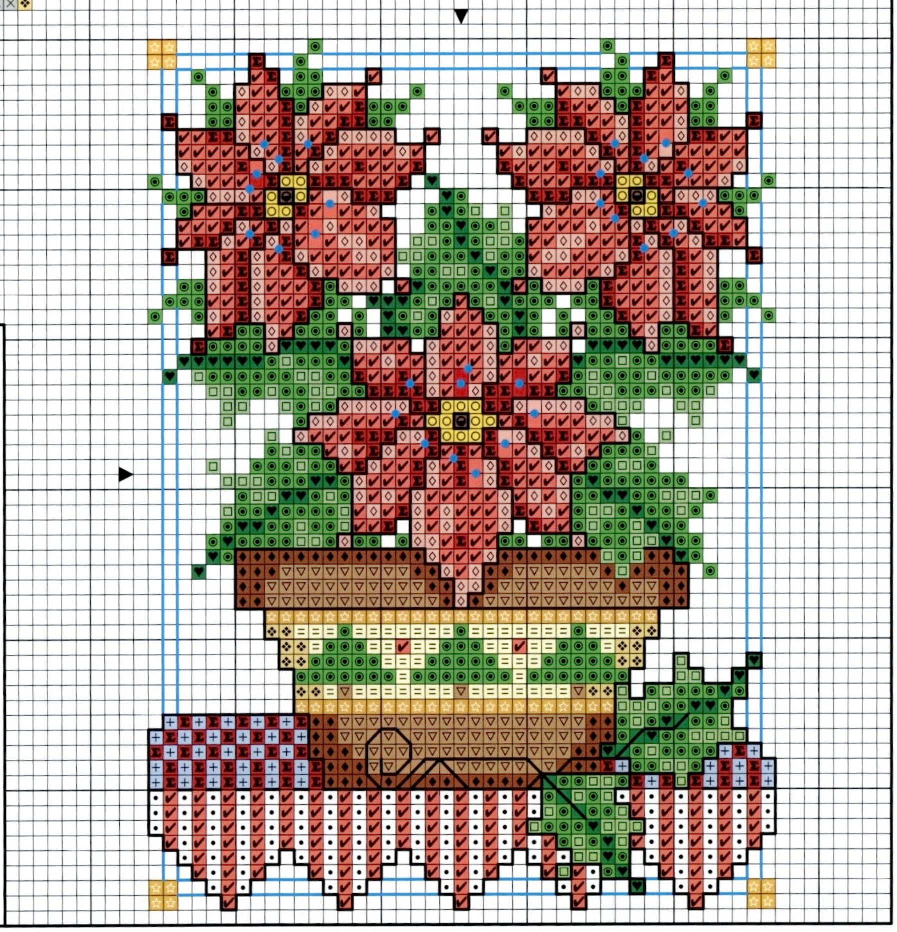

POINSETTIA (43w x 58h)

X	DMC	B'ST	ANC.	COLOR
	blanc		2	white
	350		11	coral
	352		9	lt coral
	434		310	dk tan
	436		1045	lt tan
	676		891	lt gold
	677		886	vy lt gold
	699		923	dk green
	702		226	green
	704		256	lt green
	725		305	topaz
	817		13	dk coral
	828		9159	vy lt blue
	3371		382	brown black
	3371		382	brown black Fr. Knot
				Kreinik Very Fine (#4) Braid #002 gold

PUPPY (44w x 58h)

X	DMC	1/4X	B'ST	ANC.	COLOR
	blanc			2	white
	310			403	black
	334			977	blue
	350			11	coral
	434			310	dk tan
	436			1045	lt tan
	676			891	lt gold
	699		*	923	dk green
	702			226	green
	741			304	orange
	801			359	brown
	817			13	dk coral
	976			1001	copper
	817			13	dk coral Fr. Knot
					Kreinik Very Fine (#4) Braid #002 gold

*Use long stitches for pine needles.

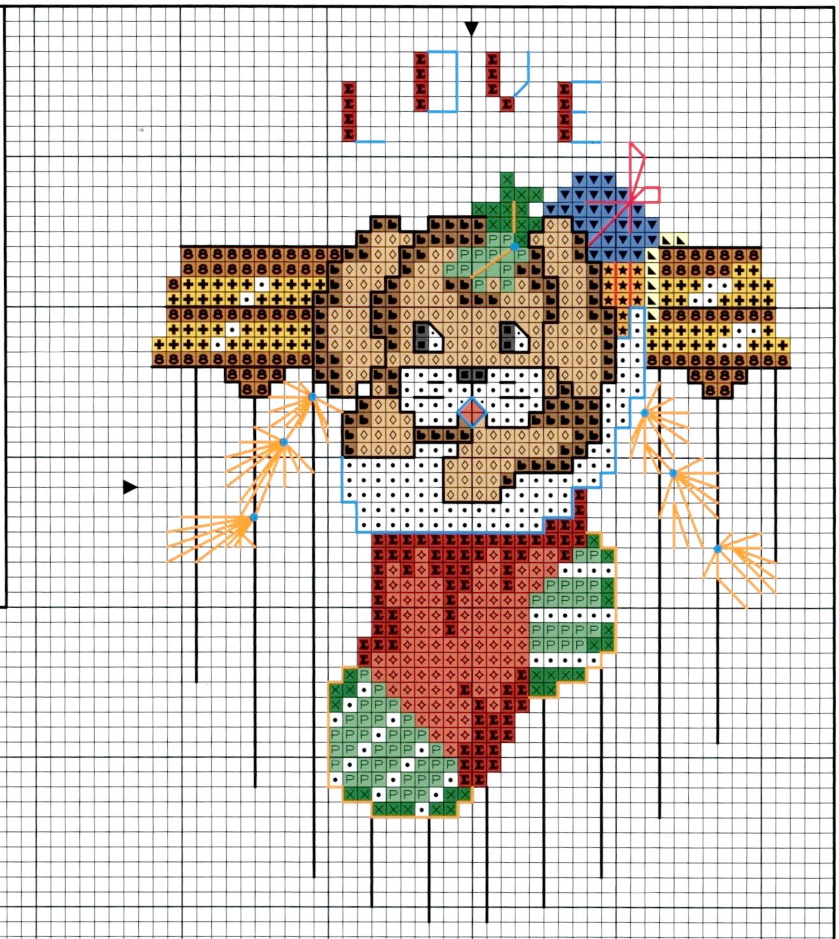

SANTA (43w x 58h)

X	DMC	1/4X	B'ST	ANC.	COLOR
	blanc			2	white
	310			403	black
	350			11	coral
	415			398	lt grey
	433			358	vy dk tan
	699			923	dk green
	702			226	lt green
	725			305	topaz
	726			295	lt topaz
	762			234	vy lt grey
	817			13	dk coral
	828			9159	vy lt blue
	898			360	dk brown
	945			881	flesh
	951			1010	lt flesh
	3326			36	pink
	310			403	black Fr. Knot
	Kreinik Very Fine (#4) Braid #002 gold				

SANTA'S BOOK (43w x 58h)					
X	DMC	¼X	B'ST	ANC.	COLOR
	blanc			2	white
	310	◩	/	403	black
	350			11	coral
	415	◩		398	lt grey
	433			358	vy dk tan
	435			1046	tan
	699			923	dk green
	702			226	green
	704			256	lt green
	725			305	topaz
	726			295	lt topaz
	762			234	vy lt grey
	817	◩		13	dk coral
	828			9159	vy lt blue
	898			360	dk brown
	945			881	flesh
	951	◩		1010	lt flesh
	3326			36	pink
	310			403	black Fr. Knot
			/	Kreinik Very Fine (#4) Braid #002 gold	

SANTA AND PUPPY (50w x 56h)				
X	DMC	B'ST	ANC.	COLOR
	blanc		2	white
	310	/	403	black
	350		11	coral
	415		398	lt grey
	676		891	lt gold
	680		901	dk gold
	699		923	dk green
	702		226	green
	704		256	lt green
	725		305	topaz
	729		890	gold
	813		161	lt blue
	817	/	13	dk coral
	945		881	flesh
	3326		36	pink
	310		403	black Fr. Knot

SANTA AND TEDDY (43w x 58h)

X	DMC	1/4X	B'ST	ANC.	COLOR
	blanc			2	white
	310			403	black
	350			11	coral
	415			398	lt grey
	699			923	dk green
	702			226	green
	704			256	lt green
	725			305	topaz
	762			234	vy lt grey
	783			307	dk topaz
	817			13	dk coral
	828			9159	vy lt blue
	945			881	flesh
	951			1010	lt flesh
	3045			888	dk yellow beige
	3046			887	yellow beige
	3047			852	lt yellow beige
	3326			36	pink
	310			403	black Fr. Knot
	Kreinik Very Fine (#4) Braid #002 gold				

SANTA AND TOY BAG (43w x 58h)

X	DMC	1/4X	B'ST	ANC.	COLOR
	blanc			2	white
	310			403	black
	350			11	coral
	415			398	lt grey
	699			923	dk green
	702			226	green
	704			256	lt green
	725			305	topaz
	762			234	vy lt grey
	783			307	dk topaz
	817			13	dk coral
	828			9159	vy lt blue
	945			881	flesh
	951			1010	lt flesh
	3045			888	dk yellow beige
	3046			887	yellow beige
	3326			36	pink
	310			403	black Fr. Knot
	Kreinik Very Fine (#4) Braid #002 gold				

X	DMC	B'ST	ANC.	COLOR
	blanc		2	white
	310	/	403	black
	350		11	coral
	676		891	lt gold
	680		901	dk gold
	699		923	dk green
	702		226	green
	704		256	lt green
	729		890	gold
	813		161	lt blue
	817		13	dk coral
	3326		36	pink
	310		403	black Fr. Knot
	350		11	coral Fr. Knot

SKATING TEDDY (44w x 58h)

TEDDY AND SOLDIER (43w x 57h)

X	DMC	1/4X	B'ST	ANC.	COLOR
	blanc			2	white
	350			11	coral
	415			398	lt grey
	699			923	dk green
	702	◩		226	green
	704			256	lt green
	742			303	dk yellow
	743			302	yellow
	798			131	royal blue
	799			136	lt royal blue
	817			13	dk coral
	828	◩		9159	vy lt blue
	945	◩		881	flesh
	3045	◩		888	dk yellow beige
	3046	◩		887	yellow beige
	3047	◩		852	lt yellow beige
	3326			36	pink
	3371	◩	/	382	brown black
	3371			382	brown black Fr. Knot
	Kreinik Very Fine (#4) Braid #002 gold				

TEDDY AND REINDEER (38w x 56h)

X	DMC	B'ST	ANC.	COLOR
•	blanc		2	white
■	310	/	403	black
✓	350		11	coral
▽	435		1046	tan
•	676		891	lt gold
⬟	680		901	dk gold
♥	699		923	dk green
◎	702		226	green
□	704		256	lt green
+	729		890	gold
=	813		161	lt blue
Σ	817	/	13	dk coral
♦	976		1001	copper
*	3326		36	pink
•	310		403	black Fr. Knot
•	817		13	dk coral Fr. Knot

TEDDY TREE (43w x 58h)

X	DMC	1/4X	B'ST	ANC.	COLOR
•	blanc			2	white
✓	350			11	coral
◒	420			374	hazel brown
◎	702			226	green
□	704			256	lt green
✦	742			303	dk yellow
○	743			302	yellow
Σ	817	◩		13	dk coral
‖	3045			888	dk yellow beige
•	3046			887	yellow beige
◇	3047	□		852	lt yellow beige
*	3326			36	pink
▼	3371		/	382	brown black
•	3371			382	brown black Fr. Knot
+	Kreinik Very Fine (#4) Braid #002 gold				

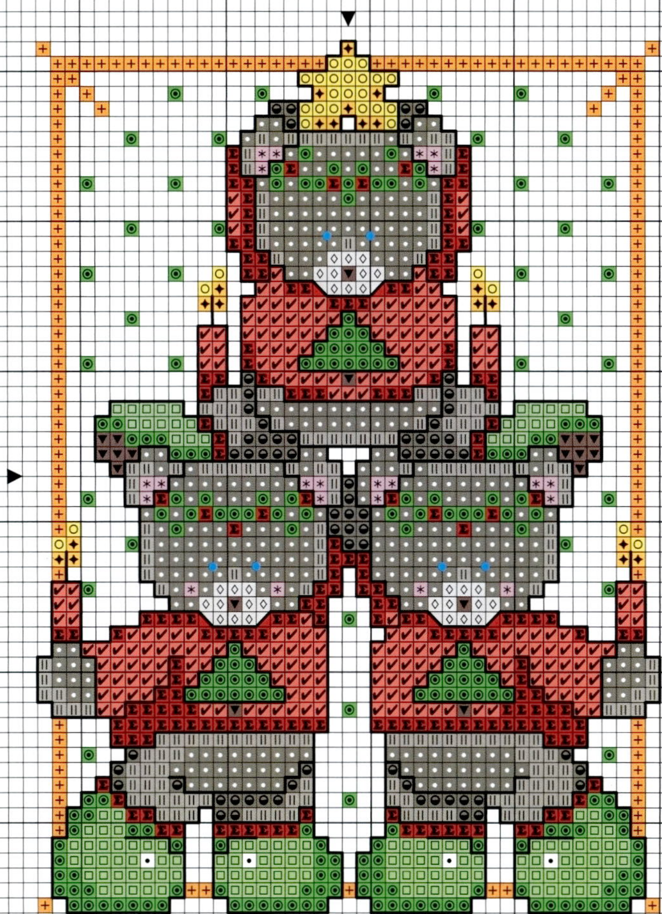

GENERAL INSTRUCTIONS

MAKING PROJECTS WITH FAST AND FESTIVE DESIGNS

These charming Christmas designs are perfect for making into a variety of creative projects. The designs in this leaflet are approximately the same size, so all you need to do is choose your favorite design, then choose your favorite finishing technique, and start stitching!

GETTING STARTED

READING CHARTS

Each of the designs is shown in chart form. Each colored square on the charts represents one Cross Stitch. Each colored triangle on the charts represents one One-Quarter Stitch or one Three-Quarter Stitch. Colored dots represent French Knots. The straight lines on the charts indicate Backstitch. When a French Knot covers a square, the symbol is omitted. When a Backstitch crosses a square, the symbol is omitted or reduced and placed on both sides of the Backstitch. When identical symbols are shown on both sides of a Backstitch, a full Cross Stitch is worked and then the Backstitch.

Each chart is accompanied by a color key. This key indicates the color of floss to use for each stitch on the chart. The headings on the color key are for Cross Stitch (**X**), DMC color number (**DMC**), One-Quarter Stitch (**$^1/_4$ X**), Three-Quarter Stitch (**$^3/_4$ X**), Backstitch (**B'ST**), Anchor color number (**ANC.**), and color name (**COLOR**). Color key columns should be read vertically and horizontally to determine type of stitch and floss color.

DETERMINING FINISHED SIZE

If you decide to stitch your design on a fabric with a different thread count than those listed in **Finishing Techniques**, use the stitch count found next to the title of the design to figure the approximate design size. Divide the number of squares (stitches) in the width of the charted design by the thread count of the fabric. For example, a charted design with a width of 80 squares worked on 14 count Aida will yield a design 5$^3/_4$" wide. Repeat for the number of squares (stitches) in the height of the charted design. (***Note:*** *To work over two fabric threads, divide the number of squares by one-half the thread count.*) Before you cut your fabric, add a generous amount to the approximate design size for finishing. Cut fabric, then begin stitching.

FINISHING TECHNIQUES

FRAME A STITCHED PIECE

Center and stitch design on a 9$^1/_2$" x 11" piece of White Aida (14 ct). Use 3 strands of floss for Cross Stitch and 1 strand for Backstitch and French Knots except where noted in color key. Use 1 strand for all stitches using Kreinik Braid. Approximate size of finished design is 3$^1/_8$" x 4$^1/_4$". Custom frame design or insert into a purchased frame when stitching is complete.

EMBELLISH A GARMENT

Use waste canvas to stitch design on a plain garment. See **Using Waste Canvas** below for instructions.

For an Adult's Garment, stitch design over a 10$^3/_4$" x 13$^1/_4$" piece of 7.5 mesh waste canvas. Use 7 strands of floss for Cross Stitch, 4 strands for French Knots, and 2 strands for Backstitch except where noted in color key. Use 3 strands for all stitches using Kreinik Braid. Approximate size of finished design is 5$^1/_8$" x 6$^7/_8$".

For a Child's Garment, stitch design over a 9" x 11" piece of 10 mesh waste canvas. Use 4 strands of floss for Cross Stitch, 3 strands for French Knots, and 2 strands for Backstitch except where noted in color key. Use 1 strand for all stitches using Kreinik Braid. Approximate size of finished design is 4$^3/_8$" x 5$^7/_8$".

Using Waste Canvas

To give a firmer stitching base when working on knit fabric, cut a piece of lightweight interfacing the same size as waste canvas. Place interfacing on wrong side of garment. Place waste canvas on right side of garment. Baste through all thicknesses. Place project in hoop; work design using a sharp needle. Trim canvas to within $^3/_4$" of design. Dampen canvas slightly to remove sizing. Use tweezers to pull out canvas threads one at a time. Trim interfacing close to design.

COVER A PHOTO ALBUM

1. Stitch the Design

Center and stitch design on a 6$^1/_2$" x 7" piece of White Aida (14 ct). Use 3 strands of floss for Cross Stitch and 1 strand for Backstitch and French Knots except where noted in color key. Use 1 strand for all stitches using Kreinik Braid. Approximate size of finished design is 3$^1/_8$" x 4$^1/_4$".

2. Mount the Stitched Piece

To pad stitched piece, cut mounting board 4" x 5$^1/_4$". Cut a paper pattern 5" x 6$^1/_4$". Centering pattern on design, cut out stitched piece. Clip $^1/_4$" into edges of stitched piece at $^1/_2$" intervals. Cut polyester bonded batting same size as board; place on board. Place stitched piece on batting; smoothly fold and glue edges to back of board.

3. Cover the Album

Cut a piece of fabric 1" larger on all four sides than open album. Cut a piece of batting same size as open album. Glue batting to outside of album. Center album, batting side down, on the wrong side of fabric. Fold and glue fabric over edges of album. For lining, cut two pieces of poster board slightly smaller than inside covers. Cut a piece of fabric 1" larger on all four sides than each poster board piece. Center poster board on wrong side of fabric. Fold and glue fabric over edges of poster board. Glue covered poster board to inside covers of album. Glue mounted stitched piece to front of photo album. Glue metallic braid around edges of mounted stitched piece. Embellish as desired to cover ends of braid.

DECORATE A PILLOW

1. Stitch the Design

Stitch 3 designs, leaving $^1/_2$" between designs, on a 15" x 9" piece of White Aida (14 ct). Use 3 strands of floss for Cross Stitch and 1 strand for Backstitch and French Knots except where noted in color key. Use 1 strand for all stitches using Kreinik Braid. Approximate size of finished design is 10" x 4$^1/_4$".

2. Cut the Fabric

For pillow front, trim stitched piece 1$^1/_2$" larger than design on all sides. Cut pillow backing same size as pillow front.

3. Make the Cording

For cording, cut a 2" wide bias strip of fabric the same measurement as outer edge of pillow front plus 3". Attach zipper foot to sewing machine. Center 1/4" diameter cord on wrong side of bias strip. Matching long raw edges, fold bias strip over cord. Gently stretching fabric as you stitch, baste next to cord. Trim seam allowance to 1/2".

4. Attach the Cording

Matching raw edges and beginning at center of one side of pillow front, pin cording to right side of pillow front. Make clips in seam allowance of cording at each corner to allow it to lie flat. Beginning and ending 2" from each end of cording, baste cording to pillow front; leave needle in fabric. Cut off one end of cording so it overlaps the other end by 1". Remove 2" of stitching from loose end of cording. Cut cord so ends butt together. Fold loose end of bias strip under 1/2"; lap it around other end. Continue stitching cording to pillow front.

5. Make the Ruffle

Cut a 5" wide bias strip of fabric two times the measurement of outer edges of pillow front. Matching right sides and short edges, use a 1/2" seam allowance to sew short edges together; press seam open. With wrong sides together, match raw edges and press ruffle in half. To gather ruffle, baste 3/8" and 1/4" from raw edge. Pull basting threads, gathering ruffle to fit edge of pillow front. Matching raw edges, pin ruffle to right side of pillow front over cording; baste in place.

6. Assemble the Pillow

Matching right sides and raw edges, use zipper foot to sew pillow front to pillow backing along stitching line, leaving an opening at bottom edge. Clip seam allowances at corners. Turn pillow right side out, carefully pushing corners outward. Stuff pillow with polyester fiberfill; sew final closure by hand.

MAKE A GIFT BAG

1. Stitch the Design

Center and stitch design on a 7 3/4" x 13 3/4" piece of White Aida (14 ct) with bottom of design 2 1/2" from one short edge. Use 3 strands for Cross Stitch and 1 strand for Backstitch and French Knots except where noted in color key. Use 1 strand for all stitches using Kreinik Braid. Approximate size of finished design is 3 1/8" x 4 1/4".

2. Cut the Fabric

After stitching is complete, trim 1" from all sides. Cut backing fabric same size as stitched piece.

3. Attach the Backing Fabric

Matching right sides and raw edges, use a 1/4" seam allowance to sew stitched piece and backing fabric together along bottom and side edges. Trim bottom corner seam allowances diagonally and press seam allowances open.

4. Finish the Gift Bag

Press top edge of bag 1/4" to wrong side; press 1/4" to wrong side again and hem. To form bottom corners, place right sides together and match side seams to bottom seam; sew across each corner 1" from end (**Fig. 1**). Turn bag right side out and press. Insert gift in bag and tie with ribbon.

Fig. 1

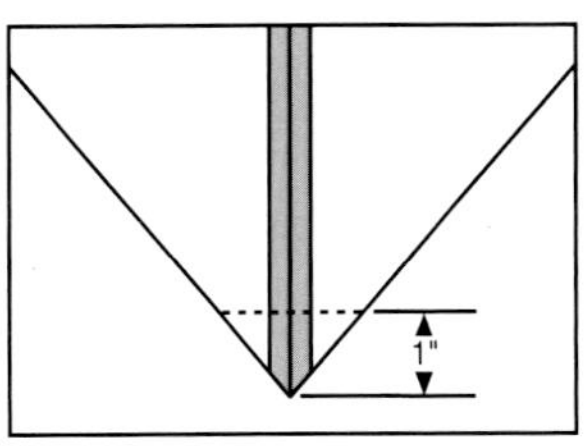

CREATE AN ORNAMENT

1. Stitch the Design

Center and stitch design on a 6 1/2" x 7" piece of White Aida (14 ct). Use 3 strands of floss for Cross Stitch and 1 strand for Backstitch and French Knots except where noted in color key. Use 1 strand for all stitches using Kreinik Braid. Approximate size of finished design is 3 1/8" x 4 1/4".

2. Cut the Mounting Board

Trace oval or rectangular pattern (page 32) onto a piece of tracing paper; cut out. Draw around pattern twice on adhesive mounting board and twice on a piece of polyester bonded batting; cut out. Adhere one batting piece to each mounting board piece.

3. Cut the Fabric

Center pattern over stitched piece; pin in place. Cut around stitched piece 1/2" larger than pattern. Cut a piece of backing fabric same size as stitched piece.

4. Attach the Stitched Piece and Backing Fabric

Center stitched piece right side up on top of batting; smoothly fold and glue edges to back of board, clipping into edges of fabric as needed. Repeat with backing fabric and remaining board piece for ornament back.

5. Make the Cording

For cording, cut a 2" wide bias strip of fabric the same measurement as outer edge of ornament plus 1". Attach zipper foot to sewing machine. Center 1/4" diameter cord on wrong side of bias strip. Matching long raw edges, fold bias strip over cord. Gently stretching fabric as you stitch, baste next to cord.

6. Attach the Cording

Beginning at bottom edge of ornament front, pin cording to wrong side of ornament front along outer edge. Make clips in seam allowance of cording to allow it to lie flat. Beginning and ending 2" from each end of cording, glue cording to wrong side of ornament front. Cut off one end of cording so it overlaps the other end by 1". Remove 1" of stitching from loose end of cording. Cut cord so ends butt together. Fold loose end of bias strip under 1/2"; lap it around other end. Glue ends in place.

7. Finish the Ornament

For hanger, glue ribbon to wrong side of ornament front at top of ornament. Glue wrong sides of ornament front and back together. Weight with a heavy book until glue is dry.

Instructions tested and photo models made by Arlene Allen, Kandi Ashford, Diane Fischer, Elaine Garrett, Arthur Jungnickel, Kellie Leonard, Sherry Merritt, Jill Morgan, Linda L. Nelson, Joyce Robinson, Susan Sego, Lavonne Sims, Carolyn Smith, Lorissa Smith, Dawn C. Speer, and Sharon Woods.

Made in U.S.A.